SCIENCE DOGS

by Meish Goldish

Consultant: Evan MacLean
Senior Research Scientist and Codirector
Duke Canine Cognition Center, Duke University

PUBLISHING

New York, New York

Credits

Cover and Title Page, © Chris Bott; Cover TR, Courtesy of Medical Detection Dogs; Cover CR, © The Washington Post/Getty Images; Cover BR, Courtesy of Medical Detection Dogs; TOC, © Mark Olencki/Wofford College; 4, © Chris Bott; 5, © Mark Olencki/Wofford College; 6, © Chris Bott; 7, © Mark Olencki/Wofford College; 8, © Bryan Meltz; 9, © Gregory Berns, How Dogs Love Us (Amazon New Harvest, 2013); 10, © Bryan Meltz; 11, © Agency-Animal-Picture/Contributor/Getty Images; 12, 13, Courtesy of Medical Detection Dogs; 14 © Robin Williams/Shutterstock; 15, © M. Cody Pickens Photography; 16, Courtesy of the University of Toronto; 17T, © Images Paediatr Cardiol. 2006 Apr–Jun; 8(2): 17–81; 17B, © Picsfive/Shutterstock; 18, 19L, © AP Photo/Michael Conroy; 19R, © AP Photo/Karen Tam; 20, © Defense Advanced Research Projects Agency; 21T, 21B, © Martin Groß; 22L, © MU Publications and Alumni Communication photo by Rob Hill; 22R, © Vadim Kozlovsky/Shutterstock; 23, © Petra Wegner/Alamy; 24, © The Washington Post/Getty Images; 25, © Artamonov Yury; 26, © David Colbran/Alamy; 27, © Thinkstock/iStockphoto; 28, © Thinkstock/Zoonar; 29TL, © Thinkstock/iStockphoto; 29TR, © Julia Remezova/Shutterstock; 29BL, © Eric Isselee/Shutterstock; 29BR, © Hemera/Thinkstock.

Publisher: Kenn Goin
Senior Editor: Joyce Tavolacci
Creative Director: Spencer Brinker
Design: Dawn Beard Creative
Photo Researcher: Picture Perfect Professionals, LLC

Library of Congress Cataloging-in-Publication Data

Goldish, Meish.
  Science dogs / by Meish Goldish.
     pages cm. — (Dog heroes)
  Audience: 7–12.
  Includes bibliographical references and index.
  ISBN-13: 978-1-61772-887-7 (library binding)
  ISBN-10: 1-61772-887-X (library binding)
  1. Dogs—Psychology—Juvenile literature. 2. Dogs—Behavior—Juvenile literature. 3. Animal models in research—Juvenile literature. I. Title.
  SF422.86.G644 2014
  636.7'0886—dc23
                              2013001908

For more information, write to Bearport Publishing Company, Inc., 45 West 21st Street, Suite 3B, New York, New York 10010. Printed in the United States of America.

10 9 8 7 6 5 4 3 2 1

Table of Contents

Memory Champ

A black-and-white border collie named Chaser sat in front of a huge pile of toys. There were more than a thousand of them. Chaser's owner, Dr. John Pilley, had spent three years trying to teach his dog the names of all the toys. Now he was ready to see if Chaser could actually remember them all.

Chaser learned the names of more than 1,000 stuffed animals, balls, and Frisbees.

To test Chaser's memory, nine toys from the pile were placed in a row. Chaser was then asked to fetch one. "Find Inky," she was told. Chaser ran to the line of toys. She looked at each one and quickly snatched up Inky, the stuffed octopus, in her mouth. Then, one by one, Chaser was told to fetch the other toys by name. The smart **canine** identified all nine objects without making a single mistake! Chaser proved that a dog can learn and remember hundreds of words.

Dr. Pilley, a retired psychologist, taught Chaser new words by showing her a toy and repeating its name up to 40 times.

Chaser was able to remember the names of 1,022 objects and could fetch each one on **command**!

Names and Actions

As Dr. Pilley taught Chaser new words, he wondered how the dog's mind worked. For example, when he said, "Fetch doll," did Chaser think the word *fetch* was part of the doll's name? Or did she understand that *fetch* was an action that she was supposed to do?

Chaser with a stuffed animal

To find the answer, Dr. Pilley taught Chaser two more action words: *paw* and *nose*. Then he told her to "Paw doll." Chaser moved the doll with her paw, but she didn't fetch it. When Dr. Pilley said, "Nose doll," the dog simply touched the toy with her nose. Chaser showed that she understood the difference between objects and actions, just as children do!

Chaser fetching a tennis ball

Chaser's ability to understand more than 1,000 words is similar to that of a three-year-old child.

Picture This

Dr. Pilley isn't the only scientist who studies how dogs' minds work. In 2012, **researchers** at Emory University in Georgia planned to use an fMRI machine to **scan** a dog's brain. They wanted to see how dogs' brains react when people give them certain signals. Dr. Gregory Berns headed the research team. He chose his own dog, Callie, for the test.

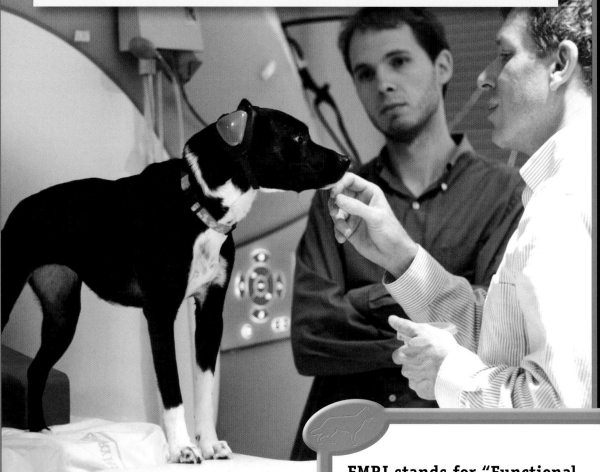

Dr. Gregory Berns (right) from Emory University with his dog, Callie, next to an fMRI machine

FMRI stands for "Functional Magnetic Resonance Imaging." The fMRI machine is a long tube that uses magnets to take videos of what's inside a body.

To prepare her for the **experiment**, Dr. Berns taught Callie two special hand signals. One signal meant she would get a tasty treat, while the other meant she would not. He also trained Callie to sit perfectly still for ten minutes. Why? For the fMRI to take clear videos of the dog's brain, Callie could not move inside the machine.

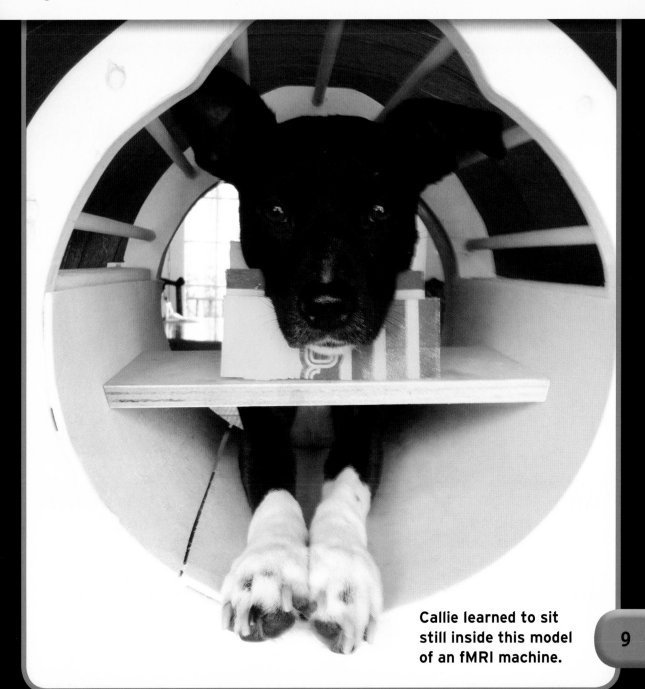

Callie learned to sit still inside this model of an fMRI machine.

Reading Signals

On the day of the experiment, Dr. Berns placed Callie inside the fMRI machine. She was then shown the two signals. As Callie watched, the machine scanned the little dog's brain to see what kind of activity was happening.

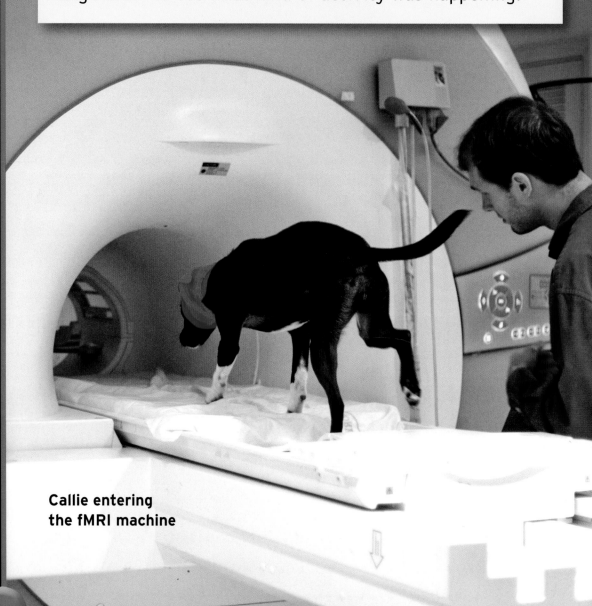

Callie entering the fMRI machine

"It was amazing to see the first brain images," said Dr. Berns. When Callie saw the "treat" signal, the fMRI showed activity in a part of her brain that processes feelings of reward. When she watched the "no treat" signal, the brain activity was missing. "I think this lets us see how dogs are responding to us," said Dr. Berns, "and that dogs pay very close attention to human signals."

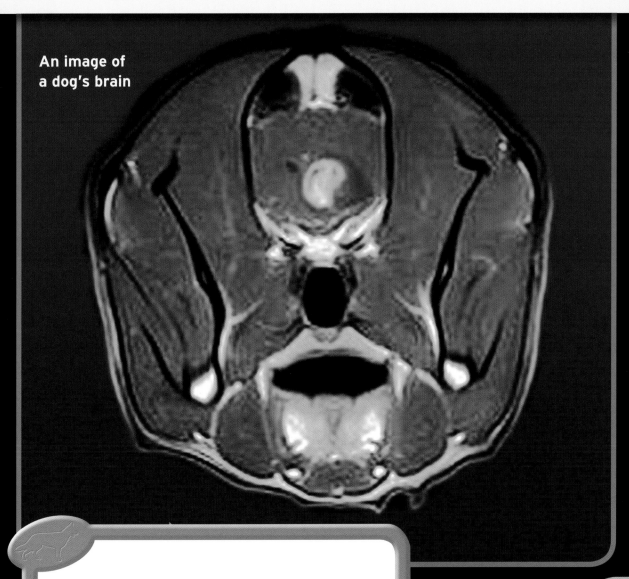

An image of a dog's brain

Emory scientists plan to use fMRI to learn what dogs think when they look at a person's face or hear a person's voice.

Cancer Detectives

Why do scientists study dogs? In some cases, understanding dogs and their super senses can help save a person's life. For example, Daisy, a Labrador retriever, has an incredible sense of smell. As a result, she was trained to use her nose to **detect** a deadly disease called cancer.

Daisy (bottom) wears a red vest that tells people that she's a cancer-detection dog.

Cancer **cells** give off certain **odors** that some dogs pick up using their powerful sense of smell. In England, there is a program called Medical Detection Dogs that trains canines like Daisy to recognize these scents. Certain dogs can detect lung or breast cancer just by smelling a person's breath. After they've found the disease, the furry detectives are trained to sit still or lie down. These signals mean, "I've found cancer!"

As part of Daisy's training, she sniffs a container that smells like cancer.

Besides sniffing for cancer, dogs have been trained to detect the odors of other things such as drugs, bombs, and bedbugs.

An Electronic Nose

Cancer-detecting dogs have inspired scientists at a company called Metabolomx to create a machine modeled after a dog's nose. Just as the sniffing cells in a dog's nose help the animal detect cancer, the Metabolomx machine picks up cancer odors. The scientists hope their "electronic nose" will be even better than a dog at detecting cancer.

A dog has 220 million sniffing cells in its nose, while a person has only about 5 million.

The Metabolomx machine looks like a computer attached to a long tube. To use the machine, a person breathes into the tube for about four minutes. Afterward, **sensors** in the machine **analyze** the person's breath for cancer odors, just as cells in a dog's nose do. Then the machine indicates whether it has found cancer on a special color-coded card.

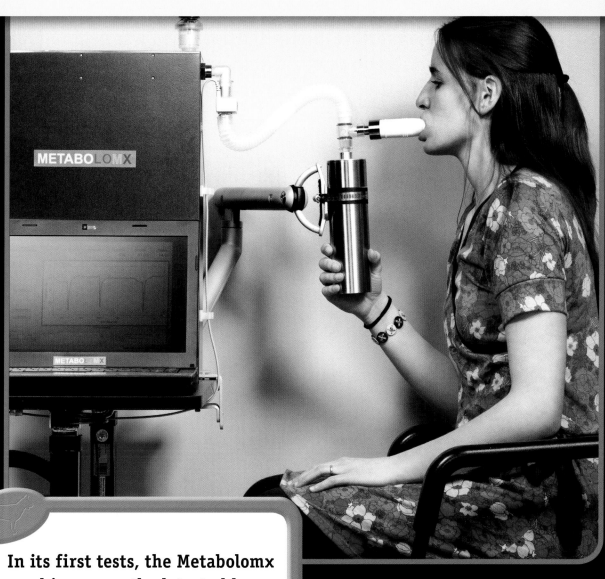

In its first tests, the Metabolomx machine correctly detected lung cancer about 80 percent of the time. Dogs are correct about 70 percent of the time.

A patient breathes into the machine, which analyzes the odors in her breath.

A Shocking Discovery

For many years, dogs have helped scientists create machines that can save lives. In the 1940s, two Canadian doctors, Wilfred G. Bigelow and John C. Callaghan, wanted to learn how to safely **operate** on a human heart. They needed to find a way to slow down the heart during **surgery**, and then restart it once the operation was over. To figure out how to do this, the doctors tested a dog to see what effects extreme cold, as well as heat from an electric shock, had on its heart.

Wilfred G. Bigelow

The results of the experiments were "a tremendous bit of good fortune," said Dr. Bigelow. The doctors found that extreme cold caused the dog's heart to stop beating. Yet the heart could be restarted and made to beat at a steady pace with jolts of electricity. Together with scientist John Hopps, the doctors used this information to develop the first pacemaker for people in 1950.

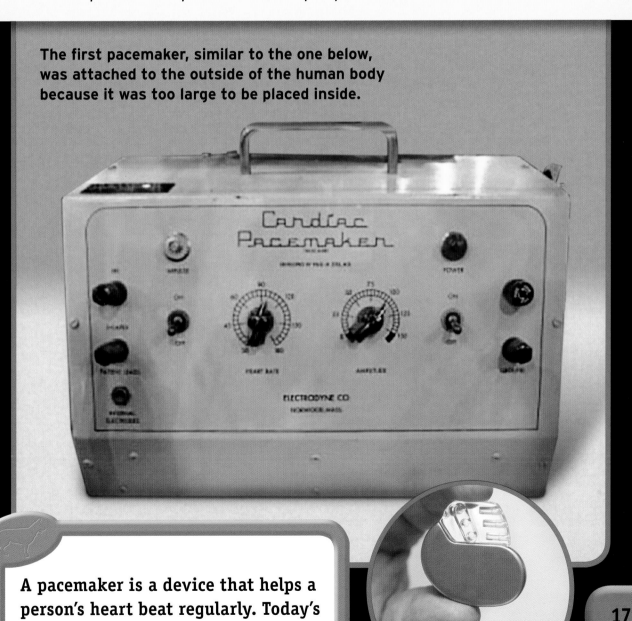

The first pacemaker, similar to the one below, was attached to the outside of the human body because it was too large to be placed inside.

A pacemaker is a device that helps a person's heart beat regularly. Today's pacemakers are so small that they can be placed inside the body.

A modern-day pacemaker

Pups with Pacemakers

Today, pacemakers aren't helping only people. Some dogs have them too! That's because dogs and humans share some of the same heart problems. Like many people, Grommit, a yellow Labrador, had a weak heart that caused him to become ill. In order to save the dog's life, doctors decided that Grommit needed a pacemaker.

Two doctors check Grommit's heart.

In 2006, Dr. Henry Green inserted a pacemaker in Grommit's neck during a two-hour surgery. Wires placed inside the dog's body ran from the **device** to Grommit's heart. Electrical signals from the pacemaker kept the Labrador's heart beating at a steady rate. After several years, the pacemaker is still working well—and Grommit is feeling better than ever!

pacemaker

A pacemaker inside a dog

Grommit after receiving his pacemaker

In the past 20 years, more than 2,000 dogs have received pacemakers.

Dogs and Robots

Scientists are also working with canines to develop machines that could help soldiers on the battlefield. In Europe, scientists want to find out how to build a four-legged robot that could still move even if it lost one of its legs in an attack.

This doglike robot climbs a small hill.

One possible use for doglike robots is to carry heavy equipment for soldiers over rugged ground.

As part of their research, scientists closely studied and filmed three-legged dogs running. They noticed that the animals ran more easily when a back leg was missing rather than a front leg. That's because canines put more weight on their front feet when they move. Scientists are using this information to build robots that can function with a missing leg as well as some dogs do!

Scientists are studying how three-legged dogs, such as this one, manage to walk and run.

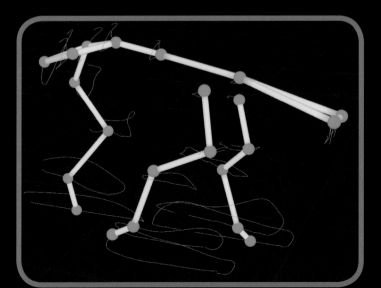

Scientists used a computer to trace the movement of a three-legged dog as it ran.

21

Sore Joints

Other scientists are also studying dogs' bodies. They want to find a way to fight **arthritis**, a painful **joint** disease that makes it hard to walk. How can studying dogs help? The knee joints of humans and dogs have similar structures and are both affected by the disease.

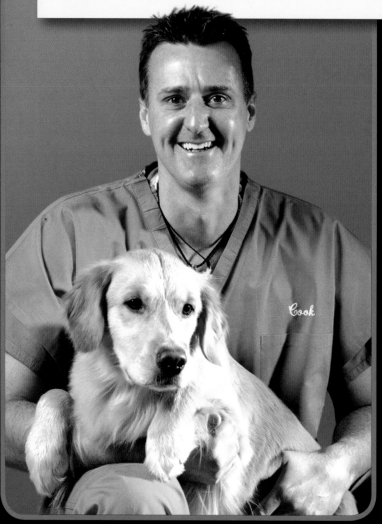

Dr. James Cook, a researcher at the University of Missouri, is studying dogs with arthritis.

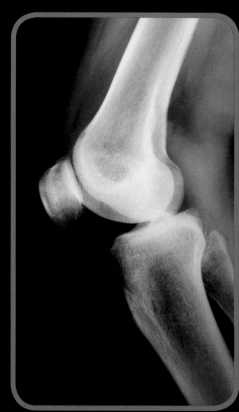

An X-ray of a person's arthritic knee joint

At the University of Missouri, researchers studied arthritis by taking a drop of blood from a dog's joint. Then they analyzed the blood's makeup. They discovered that certain chemicals were present in the blood when the dog had arthritis. The scientists' findings helped them develop a new test to detect the disease in humans, even before people feel pain in their joints.

Dogs with arthritis have trouble climbing up and down stairs.

Scientists hope the new test for arthritis will help them identify people who are at a high risk for the disease.

Miracle Walk

Scientists often work with dogs to battle health problems in humans. Yet scientists also work on behalf of canines in need. Researchers at Cambridge University in England wanted to see if they could help **paralyzed** dogs walk again. One of the dogs was a dachshund named Jasper. He couldn't use his back legs after his **spinal cord** was injured during an accident.

Just like Jasper, this dachshund is unable to move his back legs.

In 2012, the Cambridge scientists tried an unusual experiment. They took special cells from inside Jasper's nose and **transplanted** them into the damaged part of his spine. Why? Scientists knew that these cells constantly regrow to keep the nose working. Could these same cells fix a damaged spinal cord by growing inside it? The experiment worked. Four years after being paralyzed, Jasper could walk again!

Today, Jasper can walk and even swim. "It's utterly magic," said the dachshund's owner.

Jasper was part of an experiment that involved 34 dogs with spinal injuries. Many of the dogs were able to walk again after the cell transplants.

In the Future

If nose cells can fix a dog's spinal cord, what science miracles might happen next? Some answers may come from **police dogs** in Merseyside, England. After one of the dogs dies, its bones and soft **tissue** are saved in a **donor bank**. The body parts in the bank are then used to help save sick or injured pets. For example, after breaking his leg, a dog named Rusty received a new leg bone from the donor bank.

A Merseyside police dog

Rusty is one of 1,500 animals that has been saved by tissue transplants. In the future, scientists plan to perform more transplants to help canines in need. Whatever the future holds, one thing is certain: Dogs will continue to play an important part in scientific discoveries that benefit both people and animals.

Dogs can also become blood donors to help or save other dogs that have lost blood in an accident or during surgery.

Scientists work with dogs in order to help both animals and humans.

Just the Facts

- A dog smells odors up to 100 times better than a person. As a result, a dog can pick up many smells that a person can't, such as the odor given off by cancer cells.

- A beagle named Cliff has been trained to use his powerful sense of smell to detect tiny living things called bacteria that cause a deadly disease. After the dog has picked up the scent of the life-threatening bacteria in the air, he sits or lies down to let doctors know what he has found.

- The Animal Welfare Act is a law that was passed by the U.S. government in 1966. The law protects many kinds of animals, including dogs, that are part of science experiments. The act was created partly to guarantee the safety and comfort of animals that are involved in scientific research.

Any kind of dog can make a contribution to science. Here are several dog breeds featured in this book.

Border collie

Dachshund

German shepherd

Labrador retriever

29

analyze (AN-uh-lize) to examine carefully in order to learn something

arthritis (ar-THRYE-tiss) a painful disease that makes the joints in a body swollen and stiff

canine (KAY-nine) a member of the dog family, including pet dogs, wolves, and coyotes

cells (SELZ) basic, very tiny parts of a person, animal, or plant

command (kuh-MAND) an order to do something

detect (di-TEKT) to notice or discover something

device (di-VISSE) a piece of equipment that does a particular job

donor bank (DOH-nur BANGK) a place where body parts are donated and kept for future use

experiment (ek-SPER-uh-ment) a scientific test set up to find the answer to a question

joint (JOINT) a place in the body where two bones meet

odors (OH-durz) smells

operate (OP-uh-rate) to cut open a body to repair a damaged part or to remove a diseased part

paralyzed (PA-ruh-lized) unable to move

police dogs (puh-LEESS DAWGZ) dogs trained to assist the police

researchers (REE-surch-urz) people who study something in order to learn new facts about it

scan (SKAN) to examine something

sensors (SEN-surz) devices that detect or measure parts of something

spinal cord (SPY-nuhl KORD) nerve tissue that runs down a person's or an animal's back and carries messages from the brain to the body

surgery (SUR-jur-ee) an operation that treats injuries or diseases by fixing or removing parts of the body

tissue (TISH-oo) a group of similar cells that form a part of or an organ in the body

transplanted (transs-PLANT-id) took material from one body and placed it in a different body

Bibliography

Coren, Stanley. *Do Dogs Dream? Nearly Everything Your Dog Wants You to Know.* New York: W.W. Norton (2012).

Horowitz, Alexandra. *Inside of a Dog: What Dogs See, Smell, and Know.* New York: Scribner (2009).

Ritchey, David. *Why We Are Fascinated by Dogs.* Terra Alta, WV: Headline Books (2012).

Read More

Baines, Becky. *Everything Dogs: All the Canine Facts, Photos, and Fun You Can Get Your Paws On.* Washington, D.C.: National Geographic (2012).

Coile, Dr. D. Caroline. *How Smart Is Your Dog? 30 Fun Science Activities with Your Pet.* New York: Sterling (2003).

Goldish, Meish. *Dogs (Smart Animals).* New York: Bearport (2007).

Ruffin, Frances E. *Medical Detective Dogs (Dog Heroes).* New York: Bearport (2007).

Learn More Online

Visit these Web sites to learn more about science dogs:

www.medicaldetectiondogs.org.uk/

www.sciencekids.co.nz/sciencefacts/animals/dog.html

www.sciencenewsforkids.org/2012/02/no-frostbite-for-dogs-2

Index

About the Author

Meish Goldish has written more than 200 books for children.
His book *Dolphins in the Navy* received a 2012 Eureka! Honor
Book Award from the California Reading Association.